*For my dozens and dozens of wonderful cousins.*
— S.F.

Book design by Elizabeth B. Parisi

Photography by Nimkin/Parrinello and Saxton Freymann

Library of Congress Data Available

ISBN 0-439-11017-3

10 9 8 7 6 5 4 3 2 1    03 04 05 06 07
Printed in Mexico    49
First edition, September 2003

# Baby Food

ARTHUR A. LEVINE BOOKS

An imprint of Scholastic Press New York

# Puppy

**Kitten**

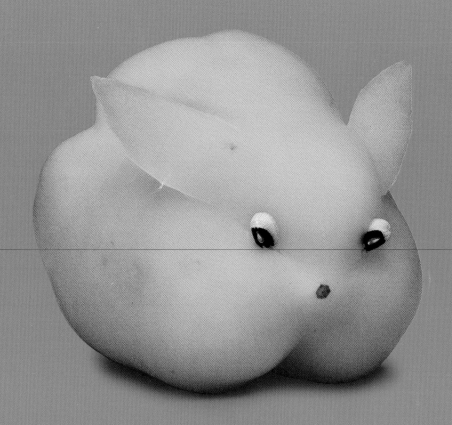

**Bunny**

**Lamb**

# Baby alligator

# Baby hippo

**Chick**

# Baby mouse

# Duckling

# Penguin chick

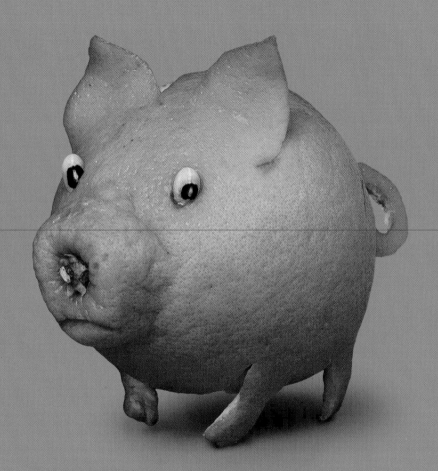

**Piglet**

# Owlet

# Kangaroo
# joey

# Seal pup

# Armadillo pup

# Lion cub

# Bear cub

# Baby monkey

**Baby giraffe**

Whale calf

# Elephant calf

**Baby octopus**

**Tadpole**

# Turtle
# hatchling

**Spiderling**

**Caterpillar**

# And me!